The Art of Fiction

The Art of Fiction

Kevin Prufer

Four Way Books
Tribeca

Library of Congress Cataloging-in-Publication Data

Names: Prufer, Kevin, author.
Title: The art of fiction / Kevin Prufer.
Description: New York : Four Way Books, [2021] | Identifiers: LCCN 2020037844 | ISBN
9781945588723 (trade paperback)
Subjects: LCGFT: Poetry.
Classification: LCC PS3566.R814 A89 2021 | DDC 811/.54--dc23
LC record available at https://lccn.loc.gov/2020037844

This book is manufactured in the United States of America and printed on
acid-free paper.

Four Way Books is a not-for-profit literary press. We are grateful for the assistance
we receive from individual donors, public arts agencies, and private foundations.

This publication is made possible with public funds from the
National Endowment for the Arts

and from the New York State Council on the Arts, a state agency,

We are a proud member of the Community of Literary Magazines and Presses.

Contents

One

Two

Three

Four

One

The Art of Fiction

In my vanished youth
I wrote a poem called "Fear of Old Age,"
in which I looked in horror on the frail bodies
of the elderly,

         the spotted hands and looming
decay,

    and that poem won a prize, $100
and the chance to read it to a half-full auditorium.

Later, in the parking lot,
a woman I'd then have called
very old told me,

        Someday
you'll understand how your poem has hurt me;
I don't expect you to get it now, but

           someday.

+

Now and then, the memory returns.

She must, I think, be
        dead by now.
She must be dead by now. And knowing this,

I can't help it: I'm smiling
because I was right to be afraid.

\+

Tonight, the internet says
they are shooting cops in Dallas. The cause
is social justice
                    and the cops are dying on the street.
Last night, cops were shooting Black people in Minneapolis
and Baton Rouge. The cause, then,
was public safety.
                    Tomorrow, we will be shooting
children in Cleveland (education), taxi drivers in Boston (traffic)
and little old ladies in St. Louis.

\+

When Antonio Jones (my childhood friend, Black)
brought his father's handgun to school,
                              all us boys crowded around.

He took it out of his knapsack
                        and its darkness glimmered.

Antonio let each of us hold it

                                awkwardly

before he slipped it into a paper bag,
and the bag into the knapsack.

                              It's cool, I said,

remembering its weight and chill in my hand.
And Antonio smiled. *Cool,* he said.

                                 And right there,

on the playground,

                        that's where the memory ends.

+

(Except all of us but Antonio were white.
This is only a fact,

like the gun in my hand was a fact,
solid and capable.)

+

The emergence of Modern Humans
from the vast networks of ancient hominids
didn't come with our discovery of tools
or even with the development of complex
language.

Rather, anthropologists now believe,
Modern Humans rose (obliterating
all other intelligent hominid species) because
of our ability to create fictions—
                              That is,
we could imagine unverifiable truths larger than ourselves—
gods, ideals, meaningful cooperations toward abstract
goals—and this allowed us to destroy
each sentient,
                    and therefore complex,
community we encountered
as we migrated out of Africa to new lands.
This, anthropologists call
                              The Cognitive Revolution.

+

The woman who hated my poem
walked toward her car with her husband.
She had entered the poetry contest,
                              but she had not won it.

Death hovered over her
like a great crow flexing its wings, its head

pivoting this way and that

                      as she walked toward her car.

+

This, anthropologists call The Cognitive Revolution:
the fiction of terror and immortality hanging over us

                                  diversely

meaningful,
five cops dead in the street because

                    how else do you respond
to a construct designed to hold vast numbers of us in fear
of death?

        An old lady trembling toward her great chariot
and out of my life.

                Tomorrow, Antonio Jones says,
holding his father's gun,

            they will kill a few more Black people.

+

But tonight

        I'm typing my memories on a glowing screen.
Apple is a fiction

          made palpable by our communal agreement

about its existence.

          Apple has workers—

many of them building machines overseas as I write.

It has advertisements.

                  Bank accounts. Accountants. A CEO.

But *Apple* itself exists only in our mutual habitation

of its fictional essence.

+

(And the iPhones that recorded the murders

of Black men in Minneapolis and Baton Rouge, that uploaded

those images to the web

                where everyone I know saw them,

are concrete expressions of the same fiction

                    we all call *Apple*).

+

Someday,

        she said,

              you will know how your poem has hurt me. Tottering

toward her great hearse

          on the far side of the Community Center.

Someday, Antonio says,

                      pocketing his father's gun,

you will wonder what became of me. Someday, you will look me up—

+

I am looking into the great glowing screen.
It's like a window I can stick my head through.

If I look long enough, I feel as though I am falling into it,
tumbling through blue force fields.

+

Google,
        a fiction that returns to its disciples
facts:
        In 1988, when we were seventeen years old,
Antonio, pursued by police
                    at high speed down Shaker Boulevard,
put his head through the windshield
                    and into the telephone pole
that also stopped his car.

+

Now what do you think of that?

                       says the old lady from the afterlife.

What do you think of that?

                  say those five dead cops

and the two dead Black men.

In order to form a more perfect fiction,

                      say the anthropologists,

though I can't tell if they're smiling, or not.

Then their cars pull from the Community Center parking lot
and disappear into the night forever—

+

and gentle Antonio walks across the playground
into memory and haze,

                his knapsack slung over one shoulder.

+

The window glows bluely into the black room
where I am forever writing my memories

                      on glass.

Fireworks

He believed that great literature was *elastic*,
and by this he meant that it shaped itself to the concerns
of each new generation of readers. Homer,
he often said, is *elastic*. We cannot read him
as Greeks, so we read him as ourselves
and find in him exactly what we are looking for.
Shakespeare. Elastic. Milton. Et cetera.

+

You're going to do it,
                              you said, and I said,
Of course I'm going to do it, and I struck the match
and for a moment
                              your face glowed yellow in its light,
and then I lit the fuse—

+

His mother had died. And later, his father had died,
painfully. So now he had no one, or so he thought.
And it was a comfort that books might speak to him
in ways that were intimate and new, that this
was part of their fundamental design,

                                          the dead
speaking to the living.

+

—and up to the heavens with the rocket
while you caught your breath
                         and the black sky ripped
with color, one rocket after another, and *Oh*, you said,
as I lit each fuse.
                    Hard to believe
the whole field would catch,
                         though it was the dry season,
late July, and the tall grasses took the flame
easily,
          and mostly I remember running from there—

+

God or his parents whispering to him through
the pages of books.
                    They spoke to him on rainless days,
his father cleaning his boots, the smell of black polish,
the sound of the brush,
                    his mother turning the page—

+

Don't move, I said, as we watched the field burn
from behind the trees—waves of gray smoke
that obliterated the barns behind them,

the circle of flame
widening. Thus the field opened
                              like an eye

+

and the young man looked up from his book.
He had read it before,
                        Achilles in the land of the dead,
mists rising off the water, the smoking dead—

What did it mean?
                        His mind
had drifted.
            His father brushing his boots until, *Darling,*
his mother said, *must you do that at the table?*
And, *Yes,* his father said, holding up the polished boot,
                                        I must.

+

It meant the following:
The wind was strong.
                    The fire devoured the field,

then it jumped to the brush by the barn,
then to the barn itself,
which caught quickly.

A single horse cowered among the hay bales,
its oily hair glowing bluely
                    as the flames approached it—

+

Calm down, you said.
                    No one will know
a thing.
          We have to get out of here
is all, and then we were running toward the car.

+

By god, I'd rather slave on earth for another man—
some dirt-poor tenant farmer who scrapes to keep alive—
than rule down here over all the breathless dead,

                             said Achilles

from the burning fields.

                      His father caught beneath the tractor's tire

gasped once more, then relaxed

                    in the field.

And now the young man was alone,

                        looking over the field

that in another part of this poem

                  I burned with my friend.

And who could account for such desolation,

reading a book by the window,
parentless and alone,

                 dry fields, perturbed by wind and sunlight—

+

And then the horse burst through the barn doors
and galloped into the field next door,

                    its flaming body

glowing orange and blue in the night,

and it set that field afire, too,
before it stumbled once, twice, and fell, smoking, onto its side—

+

and in this way, the young man thought,
laying down his book,
while his father put his boots away
and his mother sighed,
and in this way,
literature is handed on from one generation
to the next.

Archaeology

I went to the basement where my father kept his skulls.
I stood before the metal utility shelves. Skulls to the ceiling.
I looked into the eyeholes. I looked into a cranium's tomahawk hole.
Down there, it was nothing but his lab. I held
those skulls like empty pots. What did I know about Indian pots?
Some days, we went to the bars. I swung my legs from the barstool
and drank my Coke. Some days, he dug the fields.
Then it was skulls in the sink, skulls in the drying rack.
The fields are full of skulls. You have to know where the plows
turn them up. What did I know, then, about digging?
The dark inside the eyeholes. He wrote his notes on them
in indelible ink. 2.7 pounds. 2.5. The fields are full of pots.
It's true. He told me, packing his shovel into the Volkswagen.
What did I know about Indians? He kept a lab in our basement
because the university was too cheap. I went to the basement
where he kept his skulls. I looked into their eyeholes. I loved
their weight, but what did I know? When I lay in bed,
they glowed down there. It was many years ago. I closed my eyes
and the skulls talked in the basement. Indian pots. Teeth.
The noise of sex from his room. At the bars, farmers told him
what their plows turned up. I drank my Cokes. Cheap university
without a decent lab. The skulls spoke a language no one knew.
Look at this, my father said, rinsing another one in the sink.
This one took a bullet to the head. History, then, was silence.

The Damned

We could tell the saved from the damned
because,

   as the battle neared us,
the saved grew wings.

At first,

   they were barely noticeable,
two small lumps beneath a tight-fitting shirt,
invisible under a jacket.

      Months later, when the city's fall
was imminent,

    they'd grown large
and, even folded tightly,

      they poked from beneath
their coats,

   rows of neat brown feathers,
like owl feathers I remembered
from trips to the zoo with my father

      in better times.

+

One owl could turn its head
completely around,

    which astonished me,

though my father laughed at it.

It's a trick
any owl can do, he said, walking toward the egrets.

+

He didn't live to see the newspaper photo
of one egret flapping its burning wings
over the smoldering zoo,

                         or the enemy soldier
leaning against the ruined aviary

                              lighting his cigarette
and looking toward the ruins
of concession stands.

+

                    Anyway, that the saved among us
grew brown wings—some disheveled, matted—
seemed like a mercy to me,

+

though it wasn't until the battle moved
right into the heart of the city—

not until
soldiers burned the courthouse and filled the stadium
with the bedraggled and doomed—that the saved finally
took off their coats
and rose into the air.

+

My father would have been amazed
by their vast efforts,
their churning shoulders.
They might have seen more distant armies
not visible to the rest of us,
though they called down no news,
hovering instead for several minutes
before, all at once,
streaming toward the mountains.

+

That was sixty years ago. For a time, we had traces of them,
giant feathers
discovered on mountain paths—
though today no one gives them any thought,

so involved are we with the details of our lives,

we who have rebuilt our city
under a new administration.
                        Even the zoo has opened again—
busloads of schoolchildren
                        crowding at cages,
clattering strollers,
                another owl looking down on us
from the aviary.

Blueberry

She wanted to play with the blue parakeet,
so she cupped it in her hands, then let it perch
on her index finger
                until her father said the bird was tired,
dear, it gets tired, it's just a little thing,
so she made it rest an hour
                  then took it out again,
letting it balance on her shoulder. Sometimes
it tried to fly,
           but its wings had been clipped
so it fluttered to the floor and hid under the table
until she lifted it again, stroking its head,
while her father said,
              it's late now, the bird needs to sleep
and so do you.
        The bird would survive a week.

+

It is wonderful to be in love,
said the drone to its target,

but the target
was talking to his daughter.
              In love, in love, in love,

said the drone fluttering at the target's window.
It had a hot engine, a propeller's low pulse.
It took twenty pictures

                        which it sent wirelessly
to the Central Office,
pictures of a man in a well-lit dining room,
his black-haired daughter,

                        and her blue parakeet.

+

He was, the investigators believed, a very bad man,
so they observed him

                        with the attention of a lover.
Everything he said, their drone recorded, compressed,
and sent on to the Bureau

                        where such information
was processed

            for the prosecution.

+

Before she returned it to the cage,
she let the bird peck at a pile of seed
she held in her palm.

                    The bird
ate just a little. Blueberry, blueberry,
she said, stroking its feathers,
while her father
                    spoke tersely on the phone,
then studied the map
he'd spread on the table,
                    a map the little drone
tried to photograph through the window.

+

In her bedroom,
the cage was an empty head.
                    But when she opened the door
and the parakeet hopped inside,
the cage was alive with thought.

And when she covered it for the night,
the feverish cage
                    imagined first the apartment
and its tempting windows,
then the sky beyond them,

the pulse of heat on sun-dappled wings,

the vast

      and heavenward distances.

+

Darling, her father said at her bedroom door,
I've got to go out for a bit. But I'll be back very soon.

So the girl fetched the parakeet
and turned on the TV
          while the drone
followed her father down the street, hovering above his car
as he merged onto the highway—

+

          The blue parakeet balanced
on the girl's finger, looking toward the black windows.

Then it hopped onto her shoulder,
its quick little heart
        flickering in its chest. Blueberry, blueberry,
she said, posing it on the chair's back, the mantel, the book shelf,
until the bird fluttered to the floor again
and hid among the newspapers—

+

Don't forget I love you,

                the drone said as the bullet found its victim
and her father slipped the gun back into his pocket,
walking calmly down the dead man's driveway.

I love you,

        as he pulled into the street, I love you
as he turned left onto the highway ramp toward home,
the little drone

          right behind him.
Click, click, click,
said the part of its brain that takes pictures
and sends them on to the young men

              at the Central Office—

+

When he got home,

        he found his daughter asleep on the sofa,
all the lights on, the blue parakeet

           catching its breath
on the curtain rod.

        She's so light, he thought,

carrying her to bed, light as a thought.
He loved her too much.

+

And the young men at the Central Office
put away the lovesick drone.

And her father put on his pajamas
and turned out the lights.

In the middle of the night,
                                    the parakeet returned to its cage
where it knew it would be safe.

Jesus Christ

Just at that point in the play
when the dying young woman
looked into her father's eyes,
ready to tell him the truth
they both already knew
                      about the things
her dead mother had done to her,

just at that moment
of intimate silence and perhaps even
understanding
                after decades of pain,
avoidance,
           and constricted glances
over holiday dinners,

just then
           someone's cell phone rang.

+

The actors played right through the ruined moment,
while some of us in the audience turned

and the cell phone kept singing

                              into the air.

I'm sure a few of us imagined
a hapless woman rooting through her purse
desperate to turn the thing off,

                              where was it,
among the Kleenex and sunglasses, where
was it?—

+

        But when the phone finally stopped ringing
we all heard not the continuation of the scene,
but a man's voice among us saying,

                              "Look,
I can't talk right now,
I'm at a play. Yes. A *play*. I'll call you back,
ok?"

+

    And at this point, the dying young woman
got out of her hospital bed and said to the audience,
"For Christ's sake! We're working up here!"

                                                    And
we all burst into applause and boos
until an usher
                    escorted someone I could barely see—
a silhouette, really, someone in a wheelchair—
right out the back of the theater.

+

That play was one of many
we saw that last happy summer,

and the dying woman's scripted anger,
the sadnesses of unpleasant families,
were as ephemeral
                            as water
splashed on a hot sidewalk—

+

Then, I was at the funeral,
                            and the minister had just
asked us to bow our heads in silent
contemplation
                    of you, of all you meant to us,

of your many kindnesses,
before your death made a hash of those memories—
and in that moment of silence,

from somewhere
in the back of the chapel,
a cell phone

+

rang and rang—
Many of us turned around in our pews.

It was surely somewhere
by the heavy wooden doors,
where all of us had hung our winter coats

and the sound filled the chapel
the way light fills a hospital room
when, in the morning, the curtains are thrown back—

+

Then the memory of you beside me
in that dark theater,

"Jesus Christ," you'd said,

twisting around in your seat, peering
toward the back rows
                        while the cell phone
sang into the great blackness,
"Jesus Christ," all that humanity catching its breath
in the enormous theater—

+

                        And now
it was you on the stage,
reclining in your fine blue suit,

and the minister looked uncomfortable
in his high pulpit

and no one said anything at all.

The cell phone rang
                        twice more,
then abruptly hushed.

Two

The Translator

A poem in translation,

                    the young man was fond of saying,

is like the dead body of a foreigner

                        washed up on our shores.

                                     Here

he usually paused to let the metaphor sink in.

Some members of the audience nodded thoughtfully.

I will now read from my translations of a little-known ancient Roman poet,
he told them,

               shuffling his papers, then looking into

                                the dark

half-empty auditorium.

+

The dead body refused to be still. The waves
loved it too much,

               pushing it onto the beach, then rolling it
seaward again.

               And so it made its way down the beach,
alighting for a moment

                    or several moments,

                          on the wet sand,

then bobbing out

        among the American swimmers.

+

120 foreigners in a leaking boat
is too many,

        so the ocean fills with poems. Some retain
the qualities of their original language,

            but others sink
into a new language.

+

        Here I am, out here! I can see your
oil rigs glittering on the horizon,

        says the young woman whom no one
listens to. Or,

        she says nothing,
clinging to the side of the waterlogged boat,
where she has floated all night

        among the drifting bodies.

A few of them became tangled among the oil rigs,

while others arrived

        gently on our shore.

+

A poem that has floated some distance
from its accident

        transforms—so the people
ran away in horror

        when at last he came to rest
on a crowded part of the beach.

+

You foreigners in your many-sailed ships,
come join the empire! the translator intones

        from his spot-lit podium,
and the audience sighs.

        Here I am, out here,
says a little voice in the translation,

        a voice no one,
not even the translator,

        can hear.

+

The audience
had come to hear a lecture on poetry in translation

and now the translator was going on
about the ancient Roman tendency to absorb,
and therefore transform,
                    foreign cultures,
their gods and foods.

Outside the auditorium, it had grown dark,
a perfect summer night.
                    The thousand vessels
on the great black ocean
glittered and loomed

+

                    and for days, bodies
washed up on the beach.
                    Now, the American workers
zippered them into vinyl bags,

which, in the translator's metaphor,
constitutes a kind of publication.

+

But what is there to say
                               about that young woman
still clinging to the wreckage
two days into my poem?
                          A gentle summer rain
prickles her skin. *Here I am,* she says,
looking toward the oil rigs hunkering between her
and the shore.
                  Here I am.

+

She is a very fine woman
and someone should translate her.

In the Bad Days

I am writing to you
         from deep in the bad days,
hoping you will hear me
            wherever you are,
far away
     in a better time—

+

In a better time,
        hoping you will hear me,
far away,
      wherever you are:
I came upon a heron
         late at night,
deep in these bad days.

+

Late tonight,
      deep in our bad days,
he plucked a frog from the waterfilled ditch.
His eye
     was black glass. I am writing

to you,

      wherever you are

+

late in my bad days.

           The frog's neck

was broken,

        so its legs dangled.

The heron eyed me

        blackly

from the wet ditch.

         I am writing to you

+

from deep in the black days.

          The dead

dangled.

     I watched from the sidewalk.

The heron's glass eye

        eyed me

in the streetlight's glare.

         Wherever you are

+

in a better time:
people were dying.
              I am writing to tell you
people are dying.
             Remember that
while you tie your shoes
to go for your walk
              through the song-filled
night,
       through the beautiful night
in another time.

And He Will Guide My Craft

that is not a burning building it is a bonfire on the beach
and those are not soldiers they are fishermen
I am rowing us closer you will see
how those are not guns but fishing poles
a star is not a fighter plane
an island is not an aircraft carrier
and can you see the fishermen cooking their catch in the fire
I am rowing us closer
do you hear their laughter on the wind
yes it sounds like people crying but it is not
do you hear the fire popping yes it sounds like pistols
taking prisoners to the afterlife but it is not
I have always been with you
these are my hands rowing your boat
we shouldn't be on open water when the sun rises
we will dock here this is a peaceful island
you can rest you can eat
that is not smoke it is mist wrapping the cliffs
while the fishermen tend their fires
those are not bodies they are people sleeping
we will leave our boat behind when I say run
we will run as fast as we can across the sand
don't look back you will disappear into the woods
and I will disappear into your mind

Hog Kaput

Because we couldn't control their population
and because they destroyed our parks
and farm lands,
                 we proposed
to place in troughs a kind of poison
called Hog Kaput.
                   The poison, a blood thinner, killed
humanely,
             and in the video we presented to the Legislature,
the hog in the lab took only a few steps
before falling on its side.

+

              Hello,
said the feeding trough to the hungry hog.
Come here.
            At first, the hog eyed the metal trough
with suspicion. He'd grown accustomed
to the pleasures of the farmer's field
                     and that place
by the riverbank where the wild blackberry brambles
tickled his hide.
           How the sunlight dappled
the muddy water and warmed his thick neck. *C'mon,*

said the trough, and the hog

                        lumbered over,

lifted the lid with his snout, sniffed the pellets,

pushed his face inside.

\+

                    Heavy as shit, said the workman

after he'd removed the dead hog from the testing room,

hosed the floor clean,

                  and washed his hands.

Heavy as shit, he told the pregnant young woman

he'd married one year before, exactly,

                       who sat across from him

while the waiter set two bowls of soup gracefully

on the table,

             Gotta feel bad for the poor fucker,

he said,

        and she smiled because, yes, his wasn't an easy job,

but somebody, she told herself, somebody

                    had to do it.

\+

By any definition,
                    they were an invasive species,
and the citizen farmers asked only
that their lands not be disturbed.
                                        Shooting them
from helicopters
                    accomplished little—there were just
too many—
                    and even if we unintentionally
poisoned scavengers that fed on their meat,
it was a small price to pay
to keep our American parks
                                        untrammelled,
and to satisfy our farmers—

+

You see,
he told his pregnant wife,
                            the trouble is they reproduce, so two of them
become a thousand,
                            and pretty soon it's hogs everywhere,
hogs like you wouldn't believe,
                            roving gangs of hogs,
and she blew gently on the spoonful of soup,

sipped it,

        then looked up, smiling.

+

It tasted of carrot, it tasted
of wild potato, burdock root and turnip, parsnip
and sunchoke,

          and the hog ate and ate from the trough,
until he had his fill.

             Then the lid snapped shut,
and he took a step toward the river,

                  where the others
lay on the banks in sunlight,

              and from the corners of his eyes,
a delightful sparkling,

          a kind of flicker, a thousand
fireflies crowding his vision,

              beautiful, really,
and he took another step

             into what was now
a kind of snow storm—

+

So we can have meat for the table,
so we can protect the fields,
                    because some species are
invasive,
        because our country needs protection,
because we inhabit the land
the way an ideal
                inhabits the mind—
we submitted our proposal to the legislature,
hoping they would understand why it was vital that,
at all costs,
            we saw to the elimination of the hogs.

+

Yes, he said, it had been a very good meal,
a nice anniversary,
                    his wife was happy, yes, she was,
he could tell because,
                    when he helped her into the car,
then leaned inside to hand her the Styrofoam box
filled with leftovers,
                    she reached out to him,
surprised him,
            kissing him suddenly on the mouth,

and squeezing his hand.
                          So now, driving home
past the fields, now empty of hogs,
with her beside him—
                      the three of them, really,
if you counted the baby—
                         well, who could be happier
than he was?

The Vast Economies

What is the point of money? said the leopards
at work on the still quivering gazelle.

The gazelle looked at the sky, as if contemplating
the afterlife. Then it closed its eye.

All its verdant afternoons among the foliage
were not even memories anymore. Zero.

What is the point of a salary?
The camera crew, hiding in the tall grass,

recorded the scene. First there was one leopard,
then there were two. When the meat

stopped shuddering, the leopards left,
and three jackals, skulking by the waterhole,

ate next. What is the point of currency?
Zero point. Then came spotted hyenas,

white-backed buzzards, pincered water beetles.
The camera crew sat in the tall grass

eating sandwiches. They'd had a good day's work,
for which they'd be well paid.

The leopards circled them hungrily.
There are, the leopards said, economies

greater than those you think you know.
A camera remembers everything

you tell it to remember, but it has no
ideas. Now, it recorded the gazelle's bones,

mostly stripped of gore. The camera crew
packed away their equipment. The leopards

watched them closely. The gazelle
had zero left to spend.

The Newspapers

How they tumbled down the snow-filled streets,

how they slept in battered vending boxes
and hung from dowels in the public library.

How my father kept the memorable ones in his closet,
among the dying shoes.

Then the power went out. The TV closed its eye

and the house felt strange in the new silence:
a hush of snowstorm.

Because there was nothing else to do,
I went upstairs to read.

In his closet, I found an old newspaper
in a language I couldn't understand.

There he was in uniform, just below the fold—but where?
And who was that other man by his side?

I did not hear what my mother said in the kitchen
that made him throw his wine glass at her,

cutting a stain on the wall behind her head.

Let's go to the museum, my father said,
Let's get out of here.

He smelled of wine and sweat, familiar and good.

Newspapers fell from the clouds,
clotting the rooftops and the branches as we drove.

At the museum, a giant brain turned on a gear.
Press a button, he told me. *Now try another one,*

and for once I did exactly as he said.

Colored bulbs glowed on the surface,
temporal lobe, hippocampus, neural highways,

the great brain moving in the silence—

but who was that other man by his side, a rifle
propped carelessly against his shoulder?

And what had become of the gun my father held?

He was casually checking his watch.
She's cooled down by now, he said,

but I was still pressing those buttons, I couldn't stop.

Thoughts blinked on the surface,
bright networks of gold and blue,

the brain humming as it glowed in the vast gray room.

Back home, my mother wouldn't turn from the stove
or look at us. The house smelled good.

I quietly stowed the newspaper with the others, behind the shoes,
then came downstairs for dinner.

She'd cleaned the stain away.

That night, I couldn't sleep. My brain kept turning.
Pinpricks glittered like cities viewed from an airplane.

From downstairs, a muffled conversation,
then the TV changing channels

and, much later, the noise of sex.

To think he has been dead twenty years now
and she can no longer feed herself. I am 48,

typing this on a hot June night
1000 miles from there.

Rain

Before rain, the windows grew thick with fog.

Mist descended over the evening rooftops

and rain made generalities of the neighborhood.

Rain made red leaves stick to car windows.

Rain made the houses vague. A car

slid through rain past rows of houses.

The moon swiveled on a wet gear above it.

The moon—a searchlight suspended from one of the airships—

lit the vague face peering through the windshield,

the car sliding down the rain-filled darkness

toward the highway. The men controlling the airships

were searching for him,

and he passed through the rain

as a thought passes through the collective mind

of the state. Here I am in this rain-filled poem,

looking out my kitchen window into the street,

having read the news of the day—

we are hunting them in our neighborhoods,

they have no place among us—

and now the car has turned the corner and disappeared

into the searchlights that make from the rain

glittering cylinders of power.

Three

Into the Weeds

The brutality of those two men
                              who broke into her apartment
and murdered her boyfriend,
                              then, as she stepped from the shower,
shot her, too,
                   right in the face
                                    so she crumbled over the bathtub,
a little blood leaking from her mouth
                                    onto the white tiles,
has stayed with me,
                   though it was something
I saw in a film class years ago,
                              and was fictional.

+

What must it be like
for those two men
                   who, asked to get rid of a federal witness,
actually did it? I don't mean the actors,
                                    one of whom I recognized
vaguely
        from another movie,
                         but the men

61

who lived in the mind of the writer

            who created that scene?

+

I suppose it is like nothing at all to them,

            since they have exited
the writer's mind and now exist
entirely within the conventions of cinema.

            Years ago,
my professor explained it this way:

            Cinema
is committed to a pact with the audience
that allows for certain *unreal* elements

            to pass as *real*:

+

The camera following those two men
as they pocket their guns and walk toward the door—

whose perspective was that, exactly?

            And the fade-out
as we moved forward in time several weeks—

            how did that happen

in just an instant?

                    Those men lived inside

a flickering screen

+

that the rest of us can't inhabit.

But let me tell you this:

                      back when I was taking

that film course

                I had a friend named Adam. He was real,

an obsessive cyclist,

                  studied chemistry,

kept a neat row of *Star Wars* action figures

on a shelf in his dorm room—

+

then, one day,

             he died.

He was watching TV in his room,

and then he was not

                  anymore—

It was my first experience

of the death of someone
                    I loved.
I was sitting on the porch studying German verbs
when I heard.

The porch tilted entirely
                  upward
                              so I couldn't hold on,
and all of me kept tumbling
                      sideways, toward the yard—

+

He has been eighteen
and unpredictable
                for thirty years now.
                            I have many
anecdotes about him,
                which is to say he now exists
within the conventions
                of the anecdote—a funny kid
I knew
        when I was a serious kid,
                    a guy I last saw
shirtless and asleep on a sunny Tuesday

on the quad,

        making of his yellow frisbee a pillow,
while sunlight filtered through the trees
sending mottled shadows

            across his chest.

+

For the dead,

        death is the entire truth.
What else

       could there be?

But like the dead,

         those two men waiting in that woman's
apartment,

       screwing silencers onto their handguns,
also exist in the minds

       of those who remember them,

+

where the fictional and the dead
become, over time, similar.

           He was my best friend.

We sat together in film class
                    quietly making fun
of the professor
            who paced back and forth
in the lecture hall
             waving her dry erase marker over her head
talking about Scorsese's
               clever manipulation
of the passage of time
                in that scene
where the woman bleeds to death
                   on the tiles.

+

Conventions
           that make the unreal
real,
      the security distance provides—

+

It was as if the porch
           lifted up completely
and tilted sideways

and all the furniture and I

                                      tumbled over the rail

into the weeds.

In Small Spaces

The man in the apartment next door
crawled through the air conditioning duct
and made himself a space in the rafters
above her bedroom

+

and there he spent many evenings
watching her through a hole
he drilled in the ceiling.

+

One night, she sat on the bed
painting her toenails a shade of pink
he remembered years later in his prison cell.

He wrote her a letter about the color—
it was like a kitten's tongue, he said—

+

but she burned that letter in the sink,
and all the others, unopened,
having moved on with her life,

having taken a job in a new city,
married a good man, and, anyway,
that's one way into this story.

+

Don't think about the man in the rafters,
says my bottle of vodka on the coffee table.

Have another, says my empty glass.

The woman on TV with the blurred-out face says
they can't release him, she doesn't care

about his so-called rights, she's afraid
for her children, she says,
while the interviewer nods sympathetically,

+

and, have another, another,
says the bottle. Such a godless world,

and I have always wanted
someone to watch over me,

oh, gentle benignity,
the promise of drink, of blur, and

+

how he loved her, he told the TV interviewer,
in the prison's visitation room—
overwhelmingly,

+

and he didn't do anything wrong, not really,
he just looked at her, she was so beautiful,

though once or twice he removed a ceiling tile
and lowered himself into her room,

then stood over her bed
while she slept. It was nothing, really,
he never touched her,

+

except to move the hair out of her eyes
while she slept, and even then,

so gently and with loving-kindness. Stop it,

says the vodka bottle, you're inventing things,
alone here in the living room,

the television program over now,
the windows grown dark at last,

+

hard not to imagine how he brushed
that hair from her cheek,
then sat in the chair by her bed

to keep her safe the whole night long,
only crawling into the ceiling
when, toward morning, he sensed her stirring,

+

and isn't this how God works, isn't this exactly
what we expect of God, how in the world,
the vodka keeps asking me,

how in the world
is the man in this story different
from what people say about God?

Cruelties

A young man behind the garage spraying a wasps' nest
until the wasps grow heavy and dumb
dripping from the gutter
     and still he sprays
until their curled black bodies decorate the woodpile
and the nest drips poison
     while the young man smiles
is one kind of cruelty

and the cargo ship's captain throwing the castaways overboard
and though they wave their arms and call to him
he picks them off
    one by one
and only when the last one slips below her bloodcloud
does he lower his revolver
     to bow to the applauding crew
is another kind of cruelty

There is something to admire in the first cruelty
it is necessary and cultivating
     I tell myself
having moved on to the garden now
pouring poison over the fire ants' mound
spraying the hibiscus the snails were eating

but someone recorded the second cruelty on a cell phone
he'd later lose in a Bangkok taxi
so someone else could upload that video to the web
where we'd all watch it happen

                         again and again and

thank God my cruelties are small
it is impossible to tell where those stowaways died
the sea is wide open

                  there are so many people
think of the cargo ships the shipping containers

                                the economies
bright and featureless—wireless—best now
to close up the shed

                 the garden is perfect
this is a perfect garden

Wet Leaves

But by Sunday
          the old cat had slipped into a torpor
and would not move from the sofa

though the children stroked her and spoke to her softly
and gave her bits of ham,
                    which she only wheezed at.
That's how he knew it was time to put her down,
what else could he do?

+

                    Outside, the leaves fell,
ticketing the cars parked along the avenue,

sweet hum of flies over a decayed mass of leaves,
how he'd once loved autumn,
                    the smell of distant
burning, the neighborhood suffused—

+

The cat turned her green eyes
upwards
          toward the lamp-like faces

of the children bending over her,

if only she could

move her legs, if only she could float
across the room and up the stairs
as she'd done a thousand times before,
into the linen closet—

+

though it was Sunday,

and the vet closed the next day, too,
a rainy Christmas.

It seemed a cruelty

to prolong the cat's suffering until Tuesday,

he could barely stand the gasping at night,
it sounded human

+

the way his older brother fought for air

nights in the bunk above him,

that deep whistling,

even in sleep, his brother never could breathe;

finally,

he'd die of that—

+

as sometimes a falling leaf
stuck to the wet windowpane, and then another, leaves
gathering on the sill
in a light rain late in the year,
Such oak trees, he'd thought years ago,
when first he saw the house he now shared
with his two daughters
and a dying cat—

+

When the girls went to sleep at last,
he took the cat to the garage

and set her in the corner, wrapped in a blanket.
For a while, she closed her eyes and seemed to sleep,
and he was glad of that—

+

He'd made such a leafpile,
all the leaves from the yard,
and then he'd raked leaves from other yards onto a tarp
and dragged those over, too,

and all the boys leaped
into them,

and even his older brother came out
and jumped in, too—

+

The smell of rain and leaf-rot, it's the best solution,
he told himself

as he turned the engine on
and let the car idle in the closed garage.

Then, in the living room,
he poured himself a drink,

it was the most humane way,
what else could he do? And another drink—
shoot it in the head?—

as the room grew small—

+

Tommy? he'd said into the evening,
Tommy? but Tommy didn't answer,

                                 and the leafpile
loomed in the moonlight, larger now than it seemed before
and cool, and deep.

                         He was almost crying, because
he was alone,

                their parents out for dinner and Tommy
in charge, and it was so late, the leaves

                            shifting in the wind,
they shifted again,

+

the car idling in the garage,

                     how long would it take?
The sound of ice melting in his glass.

How he loved his daughters, upstairs—

+

and then there was Tommy at last
rising from the leafpile, laughing, *Scared you*, he said,
Scared you,

leaves in his hair, on his sweater,
and what could he do but pretend, *No,*
no, I was just wondering where you were,
and Tommy laughing,

> *You thought I was dead.*

+

So an hour later, when he opened the garage,
the cat wasn't on her blanket,

and it took him several minutes to find her carcass,
squeezed into the corner

> behind the rakes.

Not Thinking

When the spy shot that woman,
we both saw her last thoughts

sprayed across her car's window.
You want another glass of wine? you asked.

There was a commercial
for breath mints, then a kind of pill

to cure sadness. *Yes, thank you.*
When the show continued, that woman was not

any longer. The detective tweezed
a bit of lint from the car's seat. *Interesting,*

he said, dropping it into a plastic evidence bag.
Her empty body lay twisted in the seat.

What I meant to say is the actress held her breath
and kept perfectly still until they completed

the scene. I held my breath with her.
Once, I read that death is the absence

of thinking. You can hold your breath
all you want. That's not death.

You can tell yourself,
Think nothing. Think nothing. But, no.

The commercial for the pills comes on all the time.
In it, animated birds

fly off with another actress's sadness
until she smiles brightly. Then music.

I finished my drink
much more quickly than you did,

and poured myself two more. The detective
eventually brought his case to a conclusion,

but death lived inside the actors
even as they put on their jackets

and got into their cars. *Think nothing,*
said the ever-expanding blackness in the room.

I love you, I love you, I said,
but you were going upstairs to bed.

Then, you were not anywhere.
and the TV talked only to me.

Dignity

Don't worry, one young man
told another young man.
I'll do right by you.

But the second man
just said *No, no, no.*

Really, just hold still,
the first man said, *it'll be over in a moment.*

But he wouldn't sit still.
He tilted forward
and even tried to stand up.

This is why the bullet hit his neck
and the job was anything but quick.

If he'd held still
he'd have died with dignity.

+

The first time I fell in love
I was stupid and terrified.

The second time was dignified
and, therefore, meant to last.

The third time—

+

And he scrubbed the blood
from the table and the floor
until the kitchen winked

beneath bright windows.
And he wrapped the body

in a white sheet
and took it to the waiting car,

and laid it in the trunk.
He shouldn't've tried to get away,

the one who shot him
told the one who drove.

+

And they drove that body
from the subdivision
on the outskirts of the city

to the beautiful countryside—
gray-lit farmland, yellow
fertile light—

right into a memory
I'd put away for years,

+

a memory of telling my wife
how I felt about you.
She was angry at first,

but then she laid her head
on our kitchen table.

I wanted to write about how she cried,
but that's not the word for it.

The rasp of an old barn door
opening after many years,

and there, among the rusting tools,
the rotted hay—

+

those two men drove the body
all the way to the farmlands,

where they found an abandoned barn
on a property long forgotten
in a dust-lit clearing.

They left the body there,
behind the rotting hay bales,

where they knew no one
would soon find it. And for many years
it remained in that darkness,

unobserved, a memory
of an undignified situation

pushed to the back of the mind.

Four

I Have Voted

The dogs tipped the garbage and the meat spilled out
the larger dog sniffed it
the smaller stood to the side and growled

the meat quivered on the floor
I'd kept it too long it was
slick and fat it had expired

all this while I stood in line
and then the voting machine glowed greenly
yes yes yes I told it,

while the large dog licked the meat
lifted it gingerly with its mouth
dropped it wetly to the floor

and *America* I said walking home
from the high school gymnasium
I love you I am your son I have voted

while the two dogs circled the mess
growling oh my beautiful country a bolt gun
reduces an animal instantly

to unconsciousness no pain
says the handbook called *Bolt Stunning*
Techniques for Cattle—

Draw an X from the tops
of the eyes to the tips
of the horns the bolt goes in

there there gently
right into the skull and then we have meat
for the family for the country for the

dogs to circle I am always proud
to cast my ballot my information
into the nation's stunned skull the meat

had a suspicious smell
the little dog wouldn't stop yipping
but the larger dog had the fat pink thing in its jaws

Right in the Eye

The dogs go after the scrotum,
                         so
when they get that hog backed up against the shed,
you can walk right up with your pistol
                                   and pop him in the eye.

+

My politics are rickety.
                    They creak and shudder
like a corrugated steel shed
                         in the windstorm
yesterday evening in southwest Texas.
                                   One wild hog
got backed up against the wall
                              while the others hunkered
in the thicket.

+

        The problem with dogma
is it wants to make of complex problems
simple solutions.
            In this way, it goes after the scrotum,
the hog pressing its rump against the shed,
                                   because

what else can he do?

+

We had a problem with wild hogs. They were
overrunning the fields
                              and ruining the crops,
so we decided it would be best to kill
as many as possible,

+

                              thus sentimentality
might be the reduction of a complex political situation
to a single,
                    simplified emotional channel,
and knowing this,
                         don't look into the hog's eyes
as he backs up to the shed
                              and the dogs nip
at his flanks.

+

Last night that hog hunkered
with the other hogs
                    deep in the thicket. He was happy there.

Nearby, the rainstorm made the steel shed shudder.

After a while, he got hungry
and walked into the field
                    where the dogs were waiting.

+

Going after the scrotum
is something they just know how to do.

When they bit him, he bellowed like a man,

hating them so much he didn't see you
coming from the shadows with your pistol.

Memory

The wakeful mind
                reaches out
toward memory
                and, failing to recall,
it consults, instead,
                the internet.
So the internet becomes an extension of the mind,
                                repository
of memories the skull cannot
                contain.

+

Back then,
                it did not seem useful to me to draw
stark distinctions
                between a mind that reaches into
internal memory
                and a mind that reaches into
communal data—

+

                For instance, I was once in love
with you.

It was many years ago
and now I can't recall exactly
the shape of your lips—

how that aroused me.
When I looked for your picture on the internet,

+

I found nothing,

my memory failing me twice.
It felt, for a moment, as if you had been

entirely erased.

+

But discovering in my diary
an eloquent description of the way you leaned back on your heels
as you observed the crape myrtles

that had that morning
exploded into blossom
among the crowds by the palace,

I remembered you anew.

+

Those were the days
                                       our governing bodies
began to fail us.
                       In great paroxysms,
the citizens took to the streets.

+

                                         We stood among them,
excited by the fervor of the crowds,
the sense that we spoke
in a unified voice
                     against lawlessness,

+

and as the crowd circled the palace—
                               soldiers in green uniforms
blockading the gates
                   machine guns
propped stiffly on their shoulders—

+

you smiled, holding your phone high in the air
to upload the bodies surging toward them.

+

                              I remember
the flowering trees,
                how they swayed redly in the breeze
that cooled the city from the distant mountains.

+

I have been thinking about
repositories for memory,
                      your video
of that afternoon. My diary,
like a sleeping mind,

+

until the moment
                I opened it and discovered inside
that row of guards with their guns.
                              Then, all at once,
as if someone had given the command

directly into their nearly invisible earpieces,

                                    they pointed those guns

into the crowd

+

            where you were uploading
the demonstration.
                    How I loved you then—the crowd
surging, such laughter and upheaval,
when the bullet
                    punched through you.
Your phone
            clattered to the ground,
uploading now a chaos of feet,
                            then sky,
vaster than anything
                    you, or the crowd,
or the soldiers lowering their guns
                            in the emptying plaza,
or I,

+

at that moment crouched among strangers
behind the pock-marked church,

                              could possibly contain.

Far-Away Wars

When I was a boy,
I imagined roots

twisting around the last few landmines
buried in the orchard,

tipping them on their sides,
pushing them deeper into the soil

where their little metal brains
grew cool and corroded.

Once, I heard an explosion from those trees,
and woke to find a stump

splintered and, in places,
even charred.

Later, I learned the orchard
was to become a public park.

Now, we've rebuilt our city,
white and gleaming in the salt air.

We love its beneficence,
its avenues and beaches,

and hardly notice
that the officials we've elected

speak frequently of the dangers
of accepting refugees from warlike places.

Their boats arrive on our shores
after dark, or, with unhappy regularity,

sink, spilling bodies
that wash over our beaches.

I have always considered myself
tolerant of the lives of others,

though it disturbs me to see their faces
in line, for instance, at the grocery store.

They make me wonder
what troubles followed them,

so many minds,
the vast consciousness

of a people none of us can say
we understand,

though we wish them no particular ill.
This was not, after all, properly

an invasion. We—
I mean, my people—officially accepted them

and did our best to understand the difficulties
they'd left behind. So,

when I read that the old orchard
was finally to be converted to a civic space,

I couldn't help but recall the young trees
clutching in their roots

the last of the landmines
our fathers had planted.

Today, the shade of those trees
is cool and lavish

and we will certainly enjoy
walking new paths beneath them

at peace, all of us, though we know
those triggers are sensitive

and can withstand centuries.

Election Night

When the deified Nero
ordered Seneca to "open his veins,"
                              the playwright
complied—though he was, by then, sick and infirm
and his blood wouldn't flow quickly enough
from the wounds,
                    so his friends gave him poison
to speed his demise,
                          though this, too, failed,
and, seeing no other option, they ran a bath
for the groaning old man and finally
successfully
              drowned him in it—

+

and that is the end of Seneca who,
until then, astonished the world.

+

I was awakened late that election night
by raccoons.
              They were plundering the garbage
again, their claws scraping

inside the bins,

        the noise of ripping plastic bags.
A bottle rolled down the driveway into the grass
while I lay in bed, my book where I'd left it
under the lamp.

        Then a sudden, frantic shuffling
as they fought over, what?

        A piece of old bread,
an apple, sweet with rot—

        Beside me, my wife

never woke

+

        even when I went to the window,
moving the curtains aside,

        squinting into the dark yard
where there were so many raccoons
climbing among the garbage bins that I couldn't
count them.

+

Whether Seneca had conspired against Nero
remains an open question,

                    but his friends

had more immediate concerns.

                    The emperor had said

the old man must die,

                    and helping him on his way

was the proper thing to do,

+

                    no matter that the empire itself

was thick with rot,

                    no matter that Nero was lavish and plundering,

homicidal,

                    that he'd "lost all sense of right and wrong,

listening only to flattery,"

                    as the historian I'd been reading

that election night

                    told it. Opening his veins, she wrote,

+

was simply the best way to accomplish

                    a patriotic exit,

and the only pity was

it didn't work exactly as Seneca
had planned—

+

and what of the citizens
who took *years* to tire of Nero?
                    He had, after all,
to execute his own mother before they turned
against him—

+

                    while the raccoons scrambled in the trash,
and "Darling?" I said,
                    but my wife didn't stir,
she was dead asleep.
                    And then the raccoons
turned to face the flashlight
I aimed at them from the porch steps,
                                        their eyes reflecting
the glare greenly.

+

They froze that way—
cold air swirling,
    a night breeze
high in the trees,
    a car passing somewhere,
the darkness, for a moment,
       quiet as history,
their glowing eyes—
     before they returned to their work,

+

as, the next morning,
     I'd return to mine,
picking cold wet trash from the lawn,
       filling fresh
black bags with it,
    hosing down the driveway,

+

while my wife slept in,
and the raccoons,
    fat and satisfied, dozed
in a wet drain somewhere,

and Seneca stayed dead
in the book on the table by the bed,
                                having shown
with his friends
                a correct awareness
for the truth of power
                and the rightness of the state.

The Committee on Village Security

We locked him in a cage
and hung that cage from an old tree
down the hill from the village gate

just out of reach of the zombies
who nightly gathered below him
sucking their teeth and wailing.

He smelled good to them
and thus distracted them
from climbing the hill

and attacking us where we slept.
Mornings, we fed him and
once each week, we lowered his cage

and hosed him off. He had been
nothing but trouble to us,
and this seemed like a fair way

of putting a member
of the criminal class
to work for the public good,

though soon enough
the scent of him (and the simple fact
of vanishing populations in the hills)

brought more distant zombies to our area.
Another cage was required
to distract them

which we filled and hung
from another tree farther down the valley.
This seemed a sort of mercy.

By day the criminals might
offer each other a measure of solace,
communicating across the grassy distance,

and by night, their presence
ensured security and quality of life
for those of us in the village above them.

This was long ago.
You were young
and probably don't remember

when the village wasn't ringed
by dozens of cages. And if we have been,
of late, less solicitous

for their inhabitants'
cleanliness and welfare,
it is because these times demand it.

Of course, there are ethical considerations,
we take your point.
But the sun sets every night in the valley

and we can't avoid certain grim necessities,
even as we welcome all dissent,
productive or not—

so rest assured:
we have the community's welfare in mind,
no matter what you say,

no matter what is in your thoughts.

An American Tale

Those men heaved garbage bags onto the pyres
until the air grew thick with melting plastic
and burned meat.

              Months earlier, they'd gassed
the addled raccoons
where they crouched in the sewers

                        until yellow haze
seeped from the manhole covers
into the street.

           Later, door to door with pistols,
they found each listless cat
and put it down,

             and trucked them all to the pyres,
where they scorched the pestilence
from their fur.

           So tonight they were burning dogs—

+

A biological parasite

             might move among a population,
surviving in one host long enough
to pass itself on to multiple other hosts.

                   That was the worry,

anyway.

+

Increasingly,
scholars in the vanished Republic
                              saw cultural ideas
as a kind of virus, too. Violence, terror, fascism
incubate inside a host mind
                              that passes them on to other
susceptible minds.
                Sometimes, the host dies,
but his ideas spread among us.
                              Burning the dogs
was in some ways a literalization
                              of that.

+

Each black garbage bag
                sizzled on the flames,
then contracted suddenly
                              so I could approximate the number
of dead dogs it contained
                before the fire burned them away.

+

That the dogs were infected
                                        was an idea we got
from a report about a young girl who,
bitten in an alley,
                        behaved queerly that evening,
eventually growing listless, feverish,
and, we heard,
                        soon died.
The idea spread among us—

+

In the old days of the Republic,
I had a friend I called Charles
because I couldn't pronounce the name
his parents gave him.

Charles was a quiet boy,
fond of a neighborhood dog
                                he'd taught to sit,
roll over, play dead.
                        When his family vanished,
I'd watch that dog from my bedroom window

as it picked scraps from the neighbor's garbage.
Eventually, it, too,

          disappeared.

+

The idea was to keep some people from polluting
our country.
         The idea was they had a criminal
mentality,
      an incurable affinity for violence—
thievery, rape—that we could not tolerate
in our communities.

+

        (Charles' mother
on the front porch, sorting the day's mail
as sunlight speckled the gravel driveway;
Charles' father carrying groceries from the car
up the rain-flecked front steps.)

+

Of course,

        we could not keep a virus

from entering the Republic,

               but we could slow it

where we saw it, in our collective

                  awareness of dangerous ideas—

and so, when Charles vanished,

I sometimes fed his dog,

            until the scraps

grew so few

        no one could afford to feed any dogs.

+

Charles standing in his driveway

one snow-addled evening

            holding out a treat

until the dog finally lowered himself to the ground

and rolled quickly,

        obediently,

            onto his back.

+

The removal of some

        who lived among us

facilitated the well-being

                    of those who deserved to stay,
or so I've been told. It has been decades,
and still I miss my friend,

               whose absence
ensured the survival of the idea
of what it meant to be a citizen

                  of the vanished Republic—

+

Their shapes stand out

              in the tightening plastic
before the clarifying flames

            make ash of them.

Acknowledgments

Thanks to the editors and directors of the following publications where these poems first appeared:

Academy of American Poets' *Poem-a-Day*, *AGNI*, *Cherry Tree*, *Copper Nickel*, *Field*: *Contemporary Poetry and Poetics*, *The Gettysburg Review*, *Kenyon Review*, *Manoa*, *Paperbag*, *The Paris Review*, *Prairie Schooner*, *The Southern Review*, and *Subtropics*.

Best American Poetry 2020, edited by Paisley Rekdal (Scribner)

The Eloquent Poem, edited by Elise Paschen (Persea Press)

Poetry Society of America / Winner of the Lyric Poetry Prize: "The Newspapers"

Kevin Prufer was born in Cleveland, Ohio, and attended Wesleyan University, the Hollins Writing Program, and Washington University. He is the author of seven poetry collections, including the Four Way Books titles *How He Loved Them* (2018), winner of the Julie Suk Award, finalist for the Rilke Prize, and long-listed for the Pulitzer Prize; *Churches* (2014), named one of the ten best poetry books of the year by *The New York Times Book Review*; *In a Beautiful Country* (2011), a Rilke Prize and Poets' Prize finalist; and *National Anthem* (2008), named one of the five best poetry books of the year by *Publishers Weekly* and a finalist for the Poets' Prize. Prufer is the recipient of many awards, including four Pushcart prizes, several awards from the Poetry Society of America, fellowships from the National Endowment for the Arts and the Lannan Foundation, and several Best American Poetry selections. He teaches in the Creative Writing Program at the University of Houston and the Lesley University Low-Residency MFA Program.

Publication of this book was made possible by grants and donations. We are also grateful to those individuals who participated in our 2020 Build a Book Program. They are:

Anonymous (14), Robert Abrams, Nancy Allen, Maggie Anderson, Sally Ball, Matt Bell, Laurel Blossom, Adam Bohannon, Lee Briccetti, Therese Broderick, Jane Martha Brox, Christopher Bursk, Liam Callanan, Anthony Cappo, Carla & Steven Carlson, Paul & Brandy Carlson, Renee Carlson, Cyrus Cassells, Robin Rosen Chang, Jaye Chen, Edward W. Clark, Andrea Cohen, Ellen Cosgrove, Peter Coyote, Janet S. Crossen, Kim & David Daniels, Brian Komei Dempster, Matthew DeNichilo, Carl Dennis, Patrick Donnelly, Charles Douthat, Morgan Driscoll, Lynn Emanuel, Monica Ferrell, Elliot Figman, Laura Fjeld, Michael Foran, Jennifer Franklin, Sarah Freligh, Helen Fremont & Donna Thagard, Reginald Gibbons, Jean & Jay Glassman, Ginny Gordon, Lauri Grossman, Naomi Guttman & Jonathan Mead, Mark Halliday, Beth Harrison, Jeffrey Harrison, Page Hill Starzinger, Deming Holleran, Joan Houlihan, Thomas & Autumn Howard, Elizabeth Jackson, Christopher Johanson, Voki Kalfayan, Maeve Kinkead, David Lee, Jen Levitt, Howard Levy, Owen Lewis, Jennifer Litt, Sara London & Dean Albarelli, David Long, James Longenbach, Excelsior Love, Ralph & Mary Ann Lowen, Jacquelyn Malone, Donna Masini, Catherine McArthur, Nathan McClain, Richard McCormick, Victoria McCoy, Ellen McCulloch-Lovell, Judith McGrath, Debbie & Steve Modzelewski, Rajiv Mohabir, James T. F. Moore, Beth Morris, John Murillo & Nicole Sealey, Michael & Nancy Murphy, Maria Nazos, Kimberly Nunes, Bill O'Brien, Susan Okie & Walter Weiss, Rebecca Okrent, Sam Perkins, Megan Pinto, Kyle Potvin, Glen Pourciau, Kevin Prufer, Barbara Ras, Victoria Redel, Martha Rhodes, Paula Rhodes, Paula Ristuccia, George & Nancy Rosenfeld, M. L. Samios, Peter & Jill Schireson, Rob Schlegel, Roni & Richard Schotter, Jane Scovell, Andrew Seligsohn & Martina Anderson, James & Nancy Shalek, Soraya Shalforoosh, Peggy Shinner, Dara-Lyn Shrager, Joan Silber, Emily Sinclair, James Snyder & Krista Fragos, Alice St. Claire-Long, Megan Staffel, Bonnie Stetson, Yerra Sugarman, Dorothy Tapper Goldman,

Marjorie & Lew Tesser, Earl Teteak, Parker & Phyllis Towle, Pauline Uchmanowicz, Rosalynde Vas Dias, Connie Voisine, Valerie Wallace, Doris Warriner, Ellen Doré Watson, Martha Webster & Robert Fuentes, Calvin Wei, Bill Wenthe, Allison Benis White, Michelle Whittaker, and Ira Zapin.